STEM
IS EVERYWHERE

T0024812

JOHN LESLEY

ELECTRICITY AND MODERN
TECHNOLOGY

REDBACK
publishing

Redback Publishing
PO Box 357 Frenchs Forest NSW 2086
Australia

www.redbackpublishing.com
orders@redbackpublishing.com

© Redback Publishing 2021

ISBN 978-1-922322-59-3

Author: John Lesley
Editor: Marlene Vaughan
Designer: Redback Publishing

Original illustrations © Redback Publishing 2021
Originated by Redback Publishing

Printed and bound in China

Acknowledgements
Abbreviations: l—left, r—right, b—bottom, t—top, c—centre, m—middle
We would like to thank the following for permission to reproduce
photographs: (Images © shutterstock)

Every effort has been made to contact copyright holders of any material
reproduced in this book. Any omissions will be rectified in subsequent
printings if notice is given to the publisher.

Disclaimer
All the internet addresses (URLs) given in this book were valid at the time
of going to press. However, due to the dynamic nature of the internet,
some addresses may have changed, or sites may have changed or ceased
to exist since publication. While the author and publisher regret any
inconvenience this may cause readers, no responsibility for any such
changes can be accepted by either the author or the publisher.

MIX
Paper from
responsible sources
FSC® C020056

A catalogue record for this
book is available from the
National Library of Australia

CONTENTS

ELECTRICITY

Engineers and designers make use of electricity to create many modern technological devices.

Whether it is the mobile phone in your hand, the washing machine in the laundry, or the cars on the roads, all of these rely on electricity to work.

We know that electricity comes out of a socket in the wall, but what is it exactly, and where does it originate? Find out the answers to these and many other questions as you read through this book. At the end, you will find yourself looking at all your technological gadgets in a completely different way!

Electricity is both useful and dangerous. Used in the wrong way it can cause fires and even death. Used correctly, electricity is one of the greatest sources of energy that humans have.

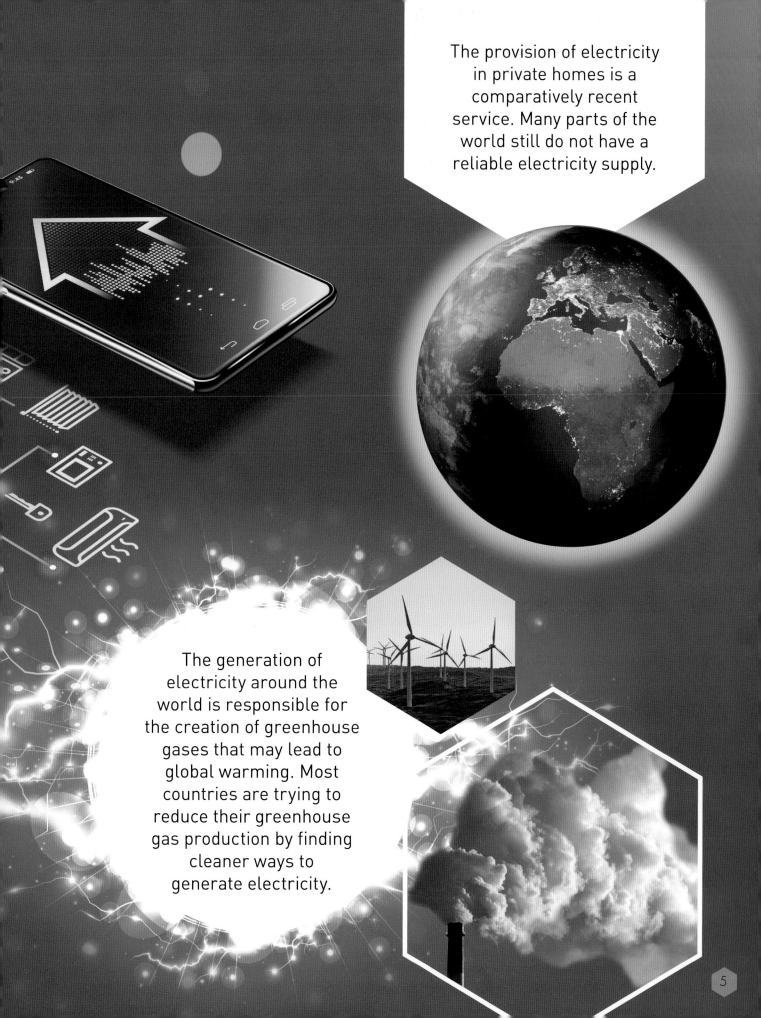

The provision of electricity in private homes is a comparatively recent service. Many parts of the world still do not have a reliable electricity supply.

The generation of electricity around the world is responsible for the creation of greenhouse gases that may lead to global warming. Most countries are trying to reduce their greenhouse gas production by finding cleaner ways to generate electricity.

HAVE WE ALWAYS HAD ELECTRICITY?

Electricity as a power source for human use is a recent discovery. Just over a hundred years ago, very few people had electrical appliances in their homes. Even electric lighting was rare. In many parts of the world, this is still the case.

For many thousands of years before people invented a way to generate electricity and send it to homes and businesses, there were other sources of power for heat, lighting and running machines. Animals made wheels turn in flour mills or on vehicles. Candles, wood, oil and coal provided lighting and heat

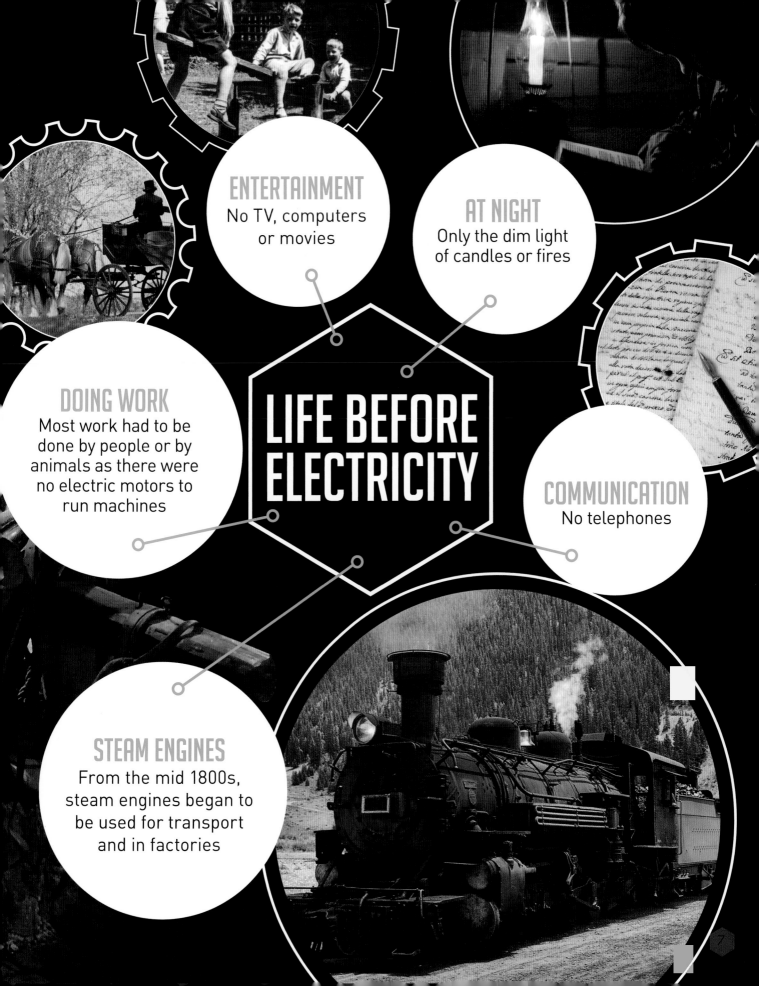

LIFE BEFORE ELECTRICITY

ENTERTAINMENT
No TV, computers or movies

AT NIGHT
Only the dim light of candles or fires

DOING WORK
Most work had to be done by people or by animals as there were no electric motors to run machines

COMMUNICATION
No telephones

STEAM ENGINES
From the mid 1800s, steam engines began to be used for transport and in factories

WHAT IS ELECTRICITY?

In our homes, electricity is the power that makes lights and all our electrical appliances work. We also know that electricity is something that can be very dangerous if we are not careful when using it.

How does an ordinary piece of wire suddenly change into a source of danger? What is the electricity that is flowing through it made of?

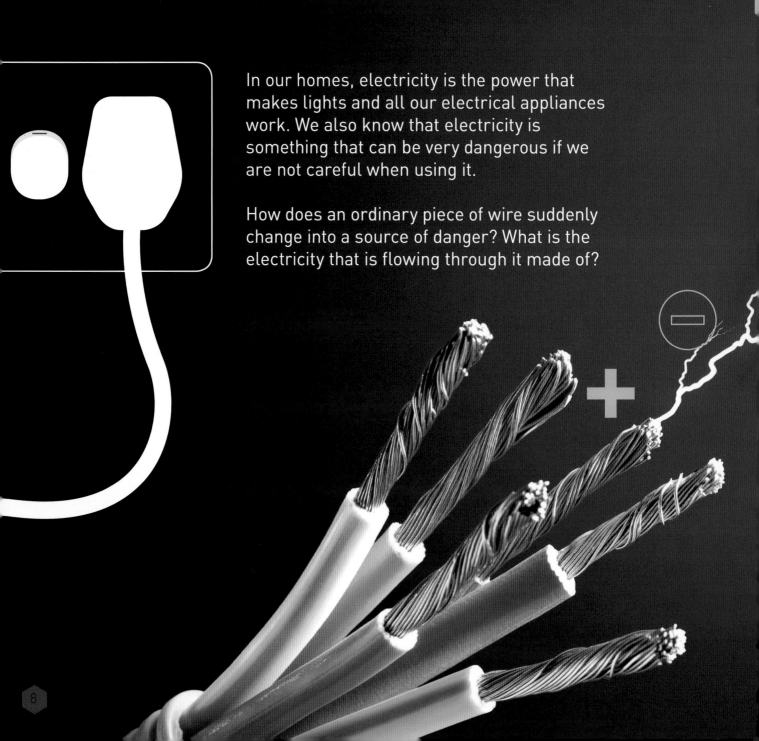

ELECTRONS

- Electricity is a flow of electrons
- An electron is a negatively charged particle
- Atoms are made of a central nucleus surrounded by one or more electrons
- When an electron escapes from its atom, it can join with many others to create a flow of electrons

ATOMS

All matter is made of atoms. Atoms have a nucleus of positively charged particles called protons, and neutral particles called neutrons. Circling around the nucleus are one or more electrons, which are negatively charged. The movement of electrons, or of their negative charge, away from their own atom can result in a flow of electricity.

ELECTRONICS

CLOSING THE CIRCUIT

Electronics is the science of electricity flowing in circuits.

Electricity needs a closed circuit to flow through appliances and make them work. In a house, the wires bringing electricity from outside form a huge loop called a circuit. To interrupt the electricity in the loop, switches break the circuit.

Once we turn on a switch, the loop is completed and electricity can flow from a wire in the wall, through the device we have plugged in, and out again through another wire. This is why there are always at least two prongs on a plug, one for the current to come out and one for it to go back again.

CURRENT THROUGH WIRE

BATTERY

CLOSED SWITCH

LAMP

SHORT CIRCUITS

If wires touch, the electricity flowing through them can cause overheating and melting. This is called a short circuit.

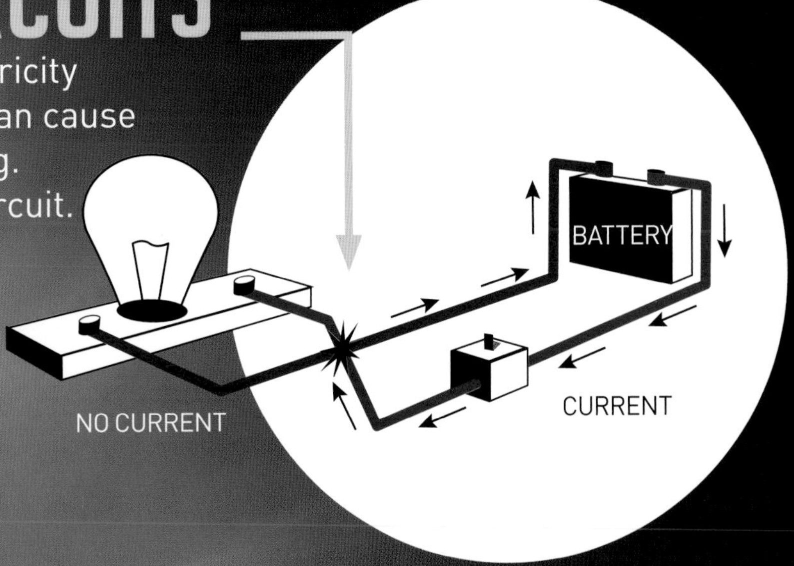

NO CURRENT

BATTERY

CURRENT

FUSES

A fuse is a thin wire that is designed to melt and break apart if there is a fault somewhere in the whole circuit. The fuse is a safety device that shuts down the flow of electricity.

FUSE

BA47-29

C16

CIRCUIT BREAKER BOX

IS THAT A CONDUCTOR OR NOT?

Electricity does not flow equally well through all materials. People who invent and design new technological devices choose which materials to use depending on how well they conduct electricity.

CONDUCTORS

These allow electricity to flow well. Conductors include metal and water.

SEMICONDUCTORS

These allow a reduced flow of electricity through them. Silicon is a semiconductor that is used in computers.

INSULATORS

These do not let electricity flow through them. Insulating materials are used to cover wires to make them safe to touch when there is electricity flowing through them. Insulators include rubber, glass and dry wood.

WHAT MAKES ELECTRICITY FLOW OUT OF A POWER POINT IN THE WALL?

Electricity in the wires in your home is waiting to leap out and start powering devices as soon as the conditions are right.

THERE ARE TWO CONDITIONS THAT NEED TO OCCUR TO MAKE THIS HAPPEN:

1

A closed circuit has to be created. This happens when we turn on the switch. The switch connects two wires allowing electricity to flow along them.

2

Electricity can only flow through materials that are conductors, such as metal wires. It cannot flow through a non-conductor, such as rubber.

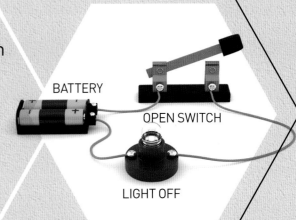

BATTERY

OPEN SWITCH

LIGHT OFF

ELECTRIC MOTORS

Electric motors are in everything from little fans, through to cars, trains and aircraft. Electric motors convert the power from electricity into a spinning force to make something turn. This could be a wheel, the plate in a microwave oven, or the blade on a circular saw.

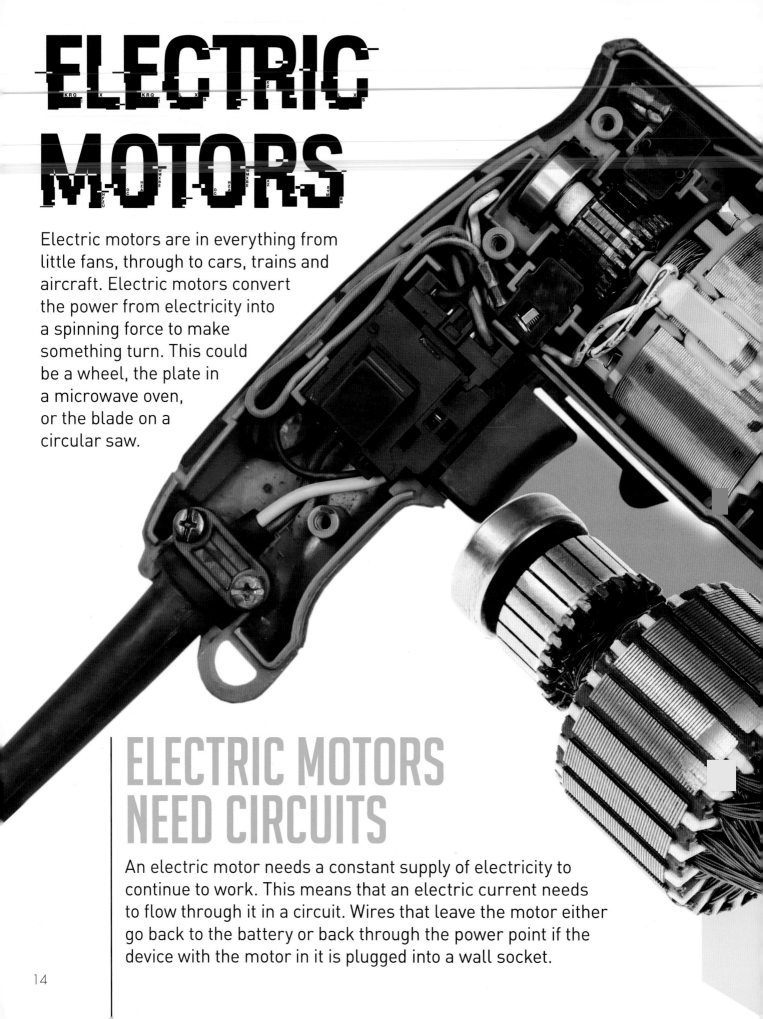

ELECTRIC MOTORS NEED CIRCUITS

An electric motor needs a constant supply of electricity to continue to work. This means that an electric current needs to flow through it in a circuit. Wires that leave the motor either go back to the battery or back through the power point if the device with the motor in it is plugged into a wall socket.

MAGNETS AND MOTORS

An electric current flowing through a wire will create a magnetic field around the wire. This magnetic attraction can be used to cause a spindle to turn. This is how the turning motion of an electric motor happens.

MAGNET

BATTERY

USING A GENERATOR TO CREATE A CURRENT

A GENERATOR IS A MACHINE THAT PRODUCES A CURRENT OF ELECTRICITY

BICYCLE LAMP

Some bicycle lamps are connected to the wheel. As the bicycle wheel turns it also turns a little generator. This creates the electric current which lights up the lamp.

- Wheel spun by tyre
- Rotating driveshaft
- Permanent magnet
- Alternating current flows through wire
- Current travels to light

GENERATORS AND MAGNETS

If a wire is made to spin near a magnet, an electric current is created in the wire. This is the basis of the generation of electricity, whether in a bicycle lamp or a gigantic generator in a power station.

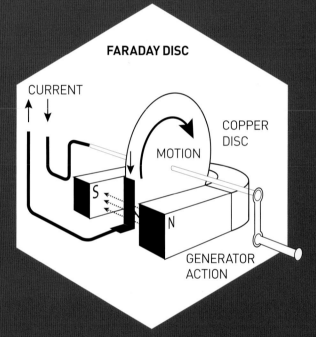

FARADAY DISC

CURRENT

COPPER DISC

MOTION

S

N

GENERATOR ACTION

POWER STATION GENERATORS

The same process used in a bicycle lamp generator is used to produce electricity in power stations. The turning motion of large machines generates electric currents that are sent along wires to where people need electricity.

FARADAY AND INDUCTION

Michael Faraday invented the first electric motor in the early 1800s. He used the word 'induction' to describe the process of creating a current of electricity using magnets and rotating copper wires.

HOW A LIGHT GLOBE WORKS

1. The base of a light globe has two metal points that connect with the electricity supply when the switch is turned on.

2. Electricity then flows through one of the wires inside the globe to the filament in the middle. The filament is usually made of very thin tungsten wire.

   The filament heats up and glows as electricity passes through it.

1. The current then leaves the light globe and flows back along the circuit.

FLOW OF ELECTRICAL CURRENT

WHEN A LIGHT GLOBE BLOWS

When a light globe blows and stops working, the inside of the glass turns black. This black substance is composed of the remnants of the broken tungsten filament.

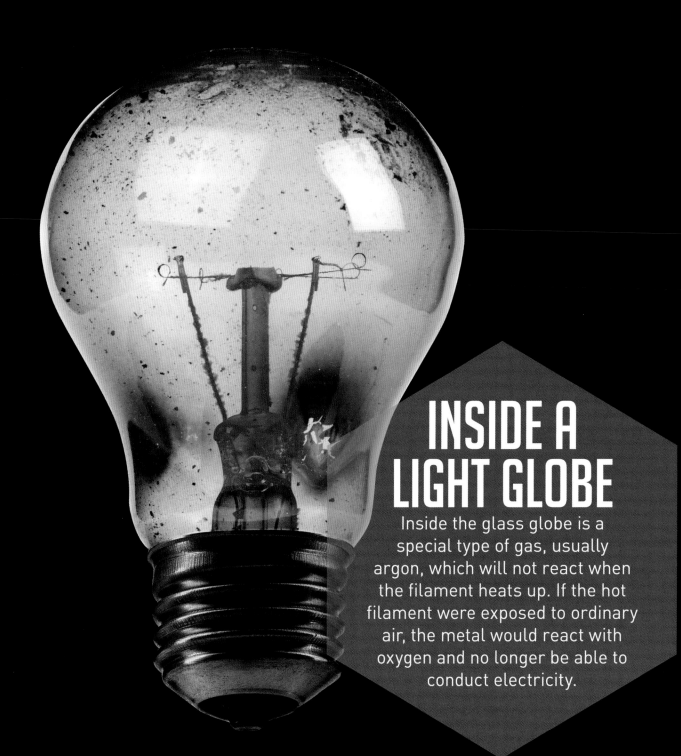

INSIDE A LIGHT GLOBE

Inside the glass globe is a special type of gas, usually argon, which will not react when the filament heats up. If the hot filament were exposed to ordinary air, the metal would react with oxygen and no longer be able to conduct electricity.

LIGHTNING

A flash of lightning happens when the energy from electricity jumps between clouds or to the ground.

STATIC ELECTRICITY

Rub some clothing together quickly and you may be able to build up a charge of static electricity. This makes a popping noise as you pull the fabric apart. In a dark room you will be able to see electric sparks jumping between pieces of the fabric. As you pull off a top made of synthetic fabric, the static electricity can make you hair stick out sideways!

ELECTRICITY IN NATURE

GLOW-WORMS

Glow-worms are insects that can create electricity in their own bodies. They use this to make a light shine from their tail.

NERVES AND BRAINS

An animal can move because its brain sends an electric signal along the nerves to make the muscles contract.

ELECTRIC EELS

Some eels can build up such a high electric charge on their bodies that any person who touches one gets a painful electric shock.

ELECTRICITY IS EVERYWHERE IN NATURE

SENSING ELECTRICITY

Sharks can detect changes in electricity in the water around them. This helps them to hunt for their food.

ELECTRICITY MADE BY PEOPLE

People make electricity by using generators. This type of electricity powers homes and factories, businesses and schools. This is also the electricity we use to charge up our mobile phones, tablets and laptops.

To make electricity, we first need a source of energy. These sources of energy are used to run the machinery that then generates the electricity and sends it through wires to where we want to use it.

SOURCES OF ENERGY FOR GENERATING ELECTRICITY

DIESEL FUEL

Diesel generators are often used to provide backup electricity for hospitals and large shopping centres in case of a power blackout.

RENEWABLE YES **NO**

COAL AND NUCLEAR FUEL

Coal and nuclear fuel are used to produce heat. The heat turns water into steam, which turns the turbines in a power station. The spinning turbines generate the electricity.

RENEWABLE YES **NO**

GEOTHERMAL

Steam from deep beneath the Earth's surface can be used to turn a turbine to generate electricity.

RENEWABLE **YES** NO

FLOWING WATER

Hydroelectricity power stations use the energy of falling water to turn turbines, which then generate the electricity.

RENEWABLE YES ~~NO~~

WAVES

The constant movement of waves can be converted by machinery into the spinning motion that a turbine needs to produce electricity.

RENEWABLE YES ~~NO~~

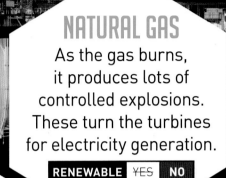

NATURAL GAS

As the gas burns, it produces lots of controlled explosions. These turn the turbines for electricity generation.

RENEWABLE ~~YES~~ NO

WIND

As a windmill turns, the motion is transferred to a generator, which produces the electricity.

RENEWABLE YES ~~NO~~

THE SUN

Solar energy comes from the Sun. It activates a solar panel, often on the roof of a building. Electrons are released from the silicon in the solar panels, and this leads to a flow of electricity.

RENEWABLE YES ~~NO~~

DELIVERING ELECTRICITY TO PEOPLE

PYLONS
Very large metal towers that carry electric wires across long distances.

A reliable electricity supply has become one of the essential services needed by society, along with water, sewerage and communication technologies. Power stations generate electricity and then send it along cables to where it is needed.

SUBSTATIONS
Places where the power of the electric current is lowered to a level that is safe to use.

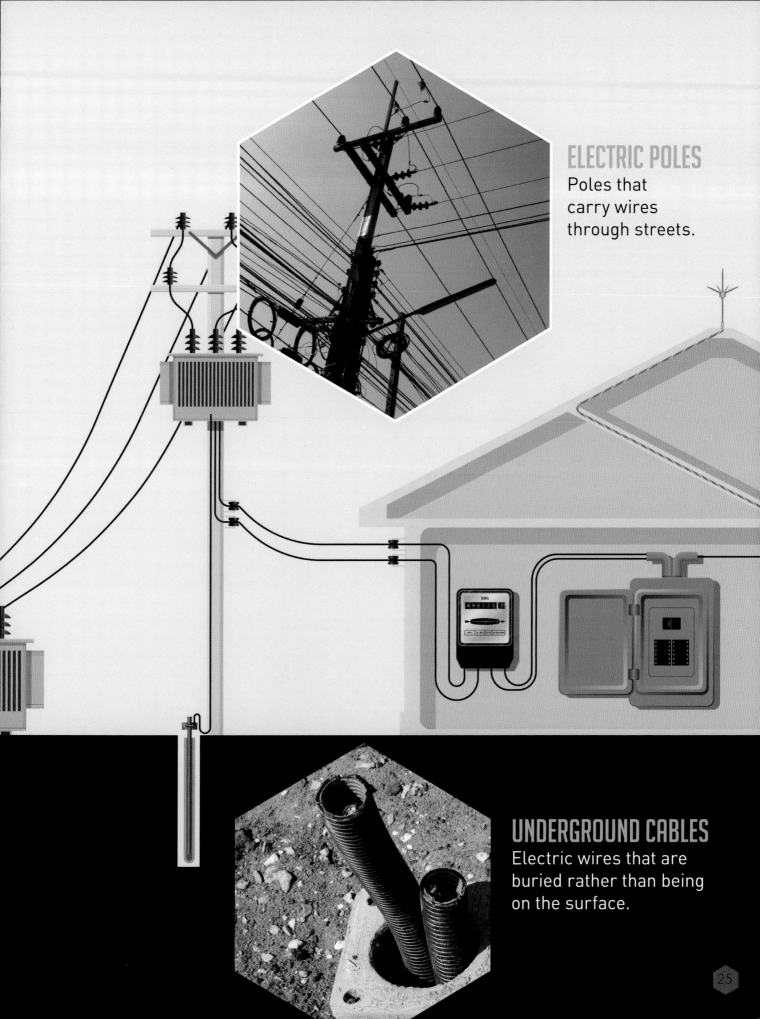

ELECTRIC POLES
Poles that carry wires through streets.

UNDERGROUND CABLES
Electric wires that are buried rather than being on the surface.

BATTERIES

Batteries can be very small, like the ones used in a TV remote controller. Batteries can also be huge and powerful enough to provide enough electricity for a small community.

A battery is full of chemicals that can store energy. This is then released as electricity when we need it. The sustainability of a rechargeable battery as an energy source depends on where the energy comes from for recharging.

Batteries may be made of chemicals that come from mining. Examples are lithium, nickel, cadmium and lead. Some contents of batteries are environmental poisons, so correct disposal of used batteries is always important.

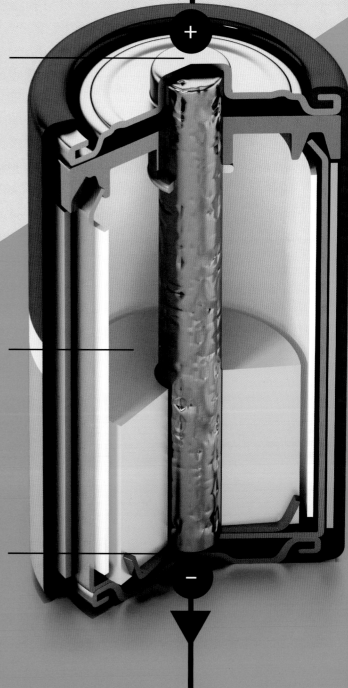

POSITIVE TERMINAL

ELECTROLYTE

NEGATIVE TERMINAL

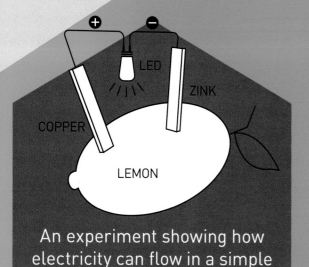

LED

COPPER

ZINK

LEMON

An experiment showing how electricity can flow in a simple battery made with a lemon!

BATTERY TERMINALS

A battery has a positive and negative terminal. When a wired circuit touches both of these terminals, electricity flows. If a globe or a toy motor is fitted somewhere along the wire, then the electricity will start doing work to turn the motor or to light the globe.

THE BAGHDAD BATTERY
WAS THIS THE FIRST BATTERY INVENTED?

Archaeologists have discovered a two thousand year old object which may be the first battery invented. It seems to be a simple battery composed of two metal plates that could have been immersed in a liquid. This is how student scientists might make a simple battery today. There is no way of knowing what this object was really used for, but the possibilities are intriguing.

SAFETY COMES FIRST!

Substations are places where extremely powerful electric currents are managed by the electricity provider. Animals that stray into a substation are sometimes killed when they touch live wires. This can also happen to people who trespass at a substation.

DANGER

SAFETY NEAR ELECTRICITY

	Keep away from electric power lines that have fallen down		Avoid being outside when there is lightning
	Never touch the battery in a car's engine as it can cause an electric shock		Do not use a hairdryer or other electric appliance near water
	Do not pull an electric appliance apart		Do not touch a power point with wet hands
	Never place any object into a toaster. The only thing that belongs there is bread		Switch a power point off before removing a plug. You might touch the metal prongs when they still have electricity running through them

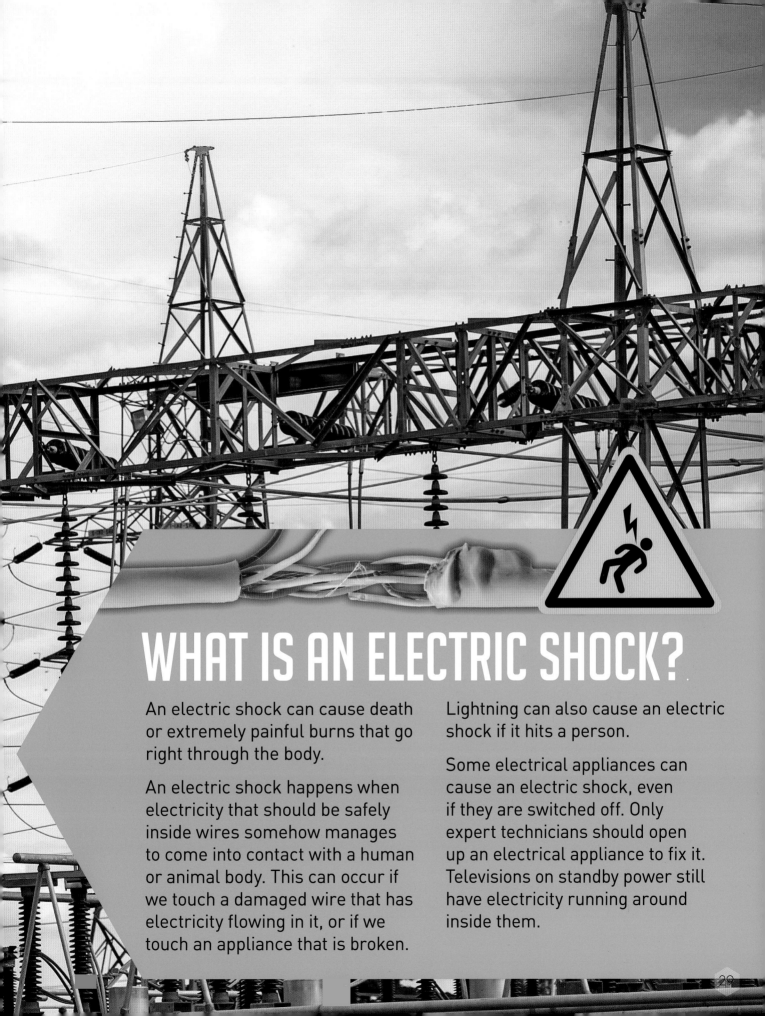

WHAT IS AN ELECTRIC SHOCK?

An electric shock can cause death or extremely painful burns that go right through the body.

An electric shock happens when electricity that should be safely inside wires somehow manages to come into contact with a human or animal body. This can occur if we touch a damaged wire that has electricity flowing in it, or if we touch an appliance that is broken.

Lightning can also cause an electric shock if it hits a person.

Some electrical appliances can cause an electric shock, even if they are switched off. Only expert technicians should open up an electrical appliance to fix it. Televisions on standby power still have electricity running around inside them.

ELECTRIC CARS

Electric cars run on electricity that comes from a battery instead of a petrol engine. The pollution from the car itself is reduced dramatically.

ENVIRONMENTALLY FRIENDLY?

An electric car is not environmentally friendly if the energy used to recharge its batteries comes from a non-renewable power source, such as coal or gas. In this case, the pollution occurs not at the car's exhaust system but at the site where the electricity is being generated.

WORDS ABOUT ELECTRICITY

argon	inert gas that does not react easily with other substances
atom	tiny particle that is the basic building block of matter
circuit	closed loop through which electricity can flow
conductor	material that allows electricity to flow through it
electron	tiny, negatively charged particle
electronics	study of electricity flowing in circuits
filament	thin piece of wire inside a light globe
fuse	tiny piece of metal designed to melt and break so that electricity stops flowing
generation of electricity	making a current of electricity flow through wires
greenhouse gas	gas such as carbon dioxide which may lead to global warming
induction	producing a flow of electricity by moving wires near magnets
insulator	material that does not allow electricity to flow through it
neutron	tiny particle without any charge
proton	tiny, positively charged particle
short circuit	occurs when two wires touch, causing overheating
switch	device that breaks a circuit, stopping the flow of electricity
tungsten	metal used to make filaments in light globes
turbine	part of a generator that turns

INDEX